to: Me from: Me

Teisha Noble

To:Me From:Me

Copyright © 2021 by Teisha M. Noble

All rights reserved. No part of this book may be reproduced or used in any manner without written permission of the copyright owner except for the use of quotations in a book review. For more information, email writersescapellc@gmail.com

Book design by David Provolo

ISBN: 978-1-7372925-0-0 (paperback)
ISBN: 978-1-7372925-3-1 (ebook)

Published by Writers Escape LLC

To the people who hurt in silent but
also love fully, smile always,
live life with a smile and always
stay positive no matter the circumstance.

Contents

SECTION 1
Inspiration

Mission Accomplished

Mission accomplished
Truth of the matter is you lose

That what happens when you try to prove
yourself and go overboard
Who are you trying to impress?
Why do you need to show off?
When you already won the prize

I tried
I cried
I was hurting myself trying to please you
You had a QUEEN
I wanted you
But
I didn't need you
I'm thriving without you

The grass isn't always greener
Is it?

Over It

All signs point to exit
As if my heart wants the curtains to close
Maybe it hurts to walk away

If I gave you the benefit of the doubt, would
our story change?

Does the good outweigh the bad?

My heart is going through these emotions
Swinging back and forth like a lost flower
in the wind

Our most valuable asset
Time
Can only heal what's damaged
I'm good

Questions

What about me?
When you hurt me
Did you realize how I would feel?

I should have known not to fall for your lies
I loved you
I gave you my all
What about me?

Now that I'm better off without you
You miss me
You needed me
But
You lost me
You got want you wanted
Didn't you?

Too Late

I tried and tried
I gave my all
And it wasn't enough
Was I ever enough?

You thought I was going to break without you?
Oh, you thought I needed you?
You thought I would beg you to come back?
Well, here's the truth

I'm glowing and growing without you
You lost something
Special
Irreplaceable
When you realize you need me it's going
to be too late

What about me?
You didn't realize my worth
I did
Now
It's too late

What about me?

Mission accomplished
Truth of the matter is you lose

That's what happens when you try to prove
yourself and go overboard
Who are you trying to impress?
Why do you need to impress them?
When you already won your prize
What about me?
When you hurt me, you didn't think about how
I would feel
I should have known not to fall for you lies

I tried and cried but I was hurting myself
trying to please you
You had a QUEEN
I wanted you but I don't NEED you
I'm special and irreplaceable
When you realize you needed me?
It was too late

You thought I was going to break without you?
Beg for you?
Surrender to you?
Well, here's the sad truth
I'm not at your command
The chapter of bowing at your feet has closed

You know what they say
You reap what you sow

Muse

I want you to touch me slowly
like you do my thighs
A whisper of a feeling that flows
through my body
A chill down my spine that only you cause
A feeling I never want to lose a love
I only get from you
A high I only feel around you a rush of emotions
I feel when I look in your eyes a place of comfort
I bask in this feeling of love only you provide

Runaway

The way you make me feel its magnetic
When we touch it's so electric
And I know only you can get me this high
High off your love

Let's run away
Go anywhere you want
I just wanna run away with you
My heart
You got it
My love
You got it
I just wanna run away with you

Just wanna keep you close to me
Never let you go
I just wanna stay here with you
Forever

SECTION 2

Racing Thoughts

Energy

It's only so much one person can take
When are you going realize that we are
all hurting?
We just mask it differently
We are here for you
Sometimes it's just too much

Positive energy is what I crave to be around
Positive energy keeps me grounded
Positive energy is what kept me going

Negative energy is .... Draining
I can't surround myself with it
The moment I sense it I need to turn it positive
When you want become stronger and positive
When you want to turn the negative to positive

I'm always here
I'm always here for you
Because
I Love You Always and Through All the Negative

Wrong

Am I doing everything wrong?
Am I saying the wrong thing all the time?
I don't understand
I just want somebody in my corner

I don't even know who you are anymore
It's always criticism
It's always the name calling
I really don't understand

I'm doing what that makes me happy
I'm trying to support myself
I'm trying to make my life better for us

How do you see me?
Am I failure to you?
Am I not enough in your eyes?
I just need to know what I'm doing wrong

Falling Apart

Nobody ever asks me how are you?
How do you feel?
I love my family I really do
But
I'm always being left out of family activities

I feel like nobody care about my feelings
I could right in front of you ready to cry
You don't say anything
Why is that?

Why can't somebody ever ask me how I feel?
Why won't you ask me if I'm okay when I'm
clearly not?
Do you even notice?

I guess not
Here I am falling apart right in front of you
And the only person that noticed isn't even in
the same city

Will you ever notice
Or
Just let me fall apart?

Feeling

I hate this feeling
The feeling of not knowing
Knowing that I can't do anything
Wishing that I could do something

I hate this hopeless feeling
I wish I could do something
I want to do something
Will it go away?

I feel so hopeless
I can't do anything
I just want something to happen
I need something to happen

I want this feeling to go away
I want things to get better
I want things to go back to how they were
I just want to be truly happy again

My Baby

Mommy wants you to know that you are
the best thing that ever happened to her
You are welcomed and loved
You took a toll on mommies' body
But I love feeling you move
Feeling your first kicks when you heard my voice

I loved watching you grow
I loved feeling you move all night when
I couldn't sleep
You are love
You are my greatest creation

I love you forever
Mommy

Never Enough

It's never enough
Whatever I do its never enough
You tell me to do something
I do it
You complain while I do
Once it's done it's still not enough

Will I ever do enough to please you?
Will I ever be enough to please you?
I don't know
I'm always doing something wrong

I really don't know what you want from me
What you expect from me
I'm trying but it's clearly not enough
I can do everything you ask
And it still won't be enough, will it?

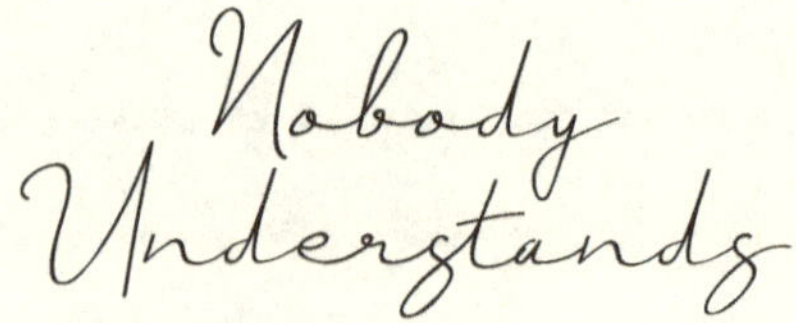

Why do I feel like my life's falling apart but coming
together at the same time?

Why do people tell me what I do wrong
but not what I'm doing right?
Why do people think it's okay to bring me down?
Why do people think it's okay to bring me down
while I'm already down?
Why do I feel like nobody understands me?
Nobody knows what's going on in my life
or just don't care to ask?

Do people know that my brother was shot in cold blood
and the night he died I thought he was coming home?
Or how painful it was to tell my cousins that the person
we did everything with had died?

Living without my brother for 16 years isn't easy
and I'm still not over it
To know that the person who taught how to ride a bike wasn't here
to see me graduate high school isn't here

I always wonder what life would be like if he was still here
But
I know if it wasn't for him, I wouldn't be where am I
or be the person I am today

Notice

I'm officially done trying to get people
to notice me
I'm not going to force myself into your life
I'm not going to beg or constantly ask you
for your time
Its draining when you care about someone
But you have to fight for their time or attention
When you say you miss me do you meant it?
Because I can't tell
Do you think about me?
Is the only time you notice me is when you see
message from me?
I really can't tell anymore
I really don't care anymore
Will you notice when I stop noticing?

Invisible

Why do I feel like I'm invisible?
Why do I feel like nobody really hears me
when I talk?
Why do I feel like in a room full of people
nobody will see me?

You only call me when you need me
to do something
Why don't you just call just to see how I am?
Ask about my feelings?
Do my feelings matter?
Or do they only matter when I'm not acting
like myself?
I just feel invisible and you only see me
when it's convenient for you

I don't know that could be a reach
But I know that my feelings are all mixed up
and nobody notices it
I don't know maybe I just need
an emotional release

Not Wanted

I can tell when I'm not wanted
I know you don't want me here and that's fine
I know you really don't like me and that's fine
But you are not going to talk to me anyway
you feel like

I don't like you either trust me I don't
But I'm not going to be disrespectful
towards you
So don't be disrespectful towards me
I'm just not going to say nothing at all to you
because I was told
If you don't have anything nice to say don't say
anything at all

One More Time

I just want to hear your voice one more time
Just want to hear you say I love you
Just want to feel your warmth when I hug you
Just want to hear you laugh when I tell
a dumb joke

Just want to hold your hand one more time
Just want to see your face when I wake up
Just want to see you smile
Just want to lay on your shoulder

Just want you to make me laugh and smile
Just want to say I love you forever
One more time

Realize

When will they realize that I will never have
what they have?
I won't have those mother-daughter talks
I won't those mother-daughter dates
I used to have that and I miss it

I feel like when my dad died, I lost a piece
of my mom
I love my family I truly do but it's not
MY family
I feel left out and like I don't belong
I feel like I'm just here

I just want things to be normal
I just want to have those moments with my mom
I want to feel a part of my family again
I just want to feel like I belong

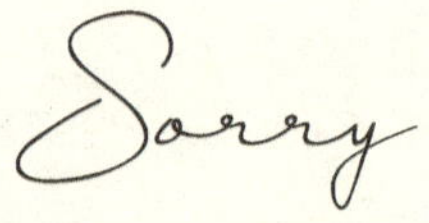

How can I not lose my confidence when I feel
like I'm being talked down by the one person
who I need to be my biggest supporter?

I keep my feeling inside which is something
I need to change
I try to say everything without being
disrespectful
Sometimes I just don't say anything at all
which is best
I don't like being compared yet I'm being
compare
I'm trying to do better for myself yet you
don't care
Then you say the worst thing a child wants
to hear
You tell me I don't have a daughter and I don't
have any children
You tell me you wish you never had me
sometimes
I done know what I did to make you feel this
way about me

I'm sorry
I'm sorry for whatever I said that made you feel
this way
I'm sorry for disrespecting you

I'm sorry for saying the wrong things
I'm sorry
I'm just sorry for everything I ever did wrong
I'm sorry for whatever I did to make you feel
this way and talk to me this way
I don't know what I did or what I didn't do
I'm deeply and truly sorry
I wish I could take it all back whatever I did
I wish I could say the things you wanted me
to say
I wish I could do the things you wanted me
to do
I wish I could be what you wanted me to be
I'm just so sorry

Strong Enough

Am I strong enough?
I keep my feelings to myself
I try to be strong
I try to keep my emotions together
But it's not working

I'm scared I'm terrified
How can I get you to understand that?
Will you understand if I tell you?
I'm trying to distract myself
It's not working

I'm still scared
I don't think I'm strong enough
I know I have God by my side always
But who is going to be my shoulder to cry on?
I hate crying

I try to surround myself with positive thoughts
Positive energy
Positive people
But something negative always creeps its way in

I may seem like I'm fine but I'm hurting and
I'm emotional drained
Nobody asks me how I feel
Do my feelings not count or matter?
Or
Am I just forgotten about?

Tired

I'm tired of being forgotten
I'm tired of being told "You should do this"
I'm tired of being questioned
I'm tired of waiting for you to come around
I'm tired of waiting for you to realize that I'm here
I'm tired of being doubted

I'm tired

I'm tired of wanting you to notice me
I'm tired of hurting
I'm tired of crying
I'm tired of being tired

I will be noticed
I will be happy
I will have somebody who thinks about me

I will be loved how I deserved be loved
I will be myself and not care what people think
I will be great

I'm just tired of
Waiting for you see that

See Me

Does anybody ever think about me?
Does anybody ever wonder about how I feel?
Nobody ever asks "What's wrong?" or
"You, okay?"
Nobody ever thinks she has been
too quiet today?
Will anybody ever ask how I'm feeling?
If you, did you would know that I'm barely here
I don't sleep
I get headaches that will sometimes last days
I'm scared to go out in case something happened
Not anything bad but something
And in the back of mind, I'm scared for you
I know you're scared but you don't express it
the right way
Nobody thinks that words hurt because we laugh
it off but sometimes, they cut deep
I know you love and care about me
But do you see me?
Your child?
Or am I just a dollar sign?
Do you see me?
Do y'all see me even as I stand in front of you
begging for you just to ask me if I'm, okay?
Maybe I'll cry when you ask
Just let me cry
Maybe I'll lie and say yeah, I'm good

Just give me a hug and tell me you love me
Maybe I'll talk
If I do just listen
That's all I want is for somebody to
See me
Listen to me
Love me

Some Days

Some days are better than others
Some days are just right but sometimes I'm off
Some days I just wanna be alone
Alone to get my thoughts together
Alone to pray
Alone to relax

Some days I'm just drained and I haven't done
anything I don't know why
I'm exhausted
I don't think I had the time to truly just stop
and be

Sometimes I just wanna sleep all day
Sometimes I feel like I'm in a dream and
I'll wake up with my mom, dad and brother
I truly feel lost

I will find myself I'm not sure when
I will be in a better space emotionally
I will become a better version of myself that
has pieces of my mom and dad

SECTION 3

Stages of Love

Heat of the Moment

In the heat of the moment, we say things
we don't mean
We hit below the belt and always go for
the jugular
But sometimes words hold more meaning than
emotions

Where do these words come from?
A place of hurt
A place of insecurity
A place of fear

Hurt that we let it get this far
Insecure with ourselves
Fear that you might leave

But what do you feel after that?
Regret
Hurt
Disbelief
We regret what we said
Hurt that maybe there is some truth in
those words
Disbelief that we actually said things
we should've

What could have stopped this situation from
getting this far?

Love should've been what stopped us
Love we have for each other
Love for the fact that we want each other
to grow
The understanding that out love should have
been stronger

Just Thought

At first, I thought you were just going to be like
any other boy I know
But then I got to know you so then that changed

That's when I started to like you and the
little things about you
But at the same time, I liked the things you said
The things you did
And that's how I caught feelings

I started to like how you would make me laugh
even if I was mad or if I was bothered
I liked how I would just smile just by talking
to you or about
I wanna say that I just started to like being with you

So, I think that if you knew this it would
change things between us
Is that true?

I just wish we were together so I can know that
all my feeling were right
Or
That you even thought about me

You

What do you say when you get asked one of
the simplest questions?
How you feel about me?
You would think that the answer would be easy
because you know exactly how you feel
It's just one problem you can't put it words
because you not used to expressing your
feelings or Because you are the one who asks
how you feel about me

I know exactly how I feel I'm just not good
with words but here goes nothing
I like how you see something in me that
I don't see in myself
No matter my mood you always find a way
to make me smile or laugh
I like your honesty
I trust you and that's rare
You just as goofy as I am

I don't know but what I do know is you make
me feel comfortable and I genuinely like you
You different a good different and I like it

Feel

I want you to know how I feel
It's just I have been hurt
I've gotten my hopes up just to be played with
But you are different
You make me feel different … In a good way

I like how you make me feel
You calm me
Make me feel comfortable
You make me laugh

I'm not sure why
But
You just make me feel good
All I know is I like what we have
It keeps me calm and happy
I'm trying to … open up
Just
Give me time

I care about you too much just to let you go now

If Only

If only you knew how I really feel about you
If you knew what was going through my mind
You would be shocked

If you knew that when I see you for some reason,
I get butterflies
When you talk to me, I can't find the right word
to say

If you knew that even if I see or talk to you,
I still think about you
Weird

If you knew that when you touch me, I get chills
Sometimes when you touch me, I have to
control myself because
I don't know what I would do if I didn't

Sometimes I just want to grab you and kiss you
but who knows what that might lead to
So, if you knew all this
How would you feel?
What would say or do?

Somebody

I want somebody that calls just to hear my voice
I want somebody who checks up on me
I want somebody make sure I'm okay mentally
I want somebody that plans random dates

I want somebody spontaneous and fun
I want somebody who can just make me happy
by being there
Call me and tell me you love me
Pick me up just because you want to sit and talk
Look at me and tell me I'm beautiful just
because
Hold me when I need comfort
Show me off just because you're happy to be
with me

Somebody who makes me feel like I'm the
best thing that happened to them

What to do

I won't never be enough for you
I can't say I love you enough because you don't
believe it
I don't know what to do or say
And even if I think it's the right thing you never
listen and its always the wrong thing
I'm confused and hurt
How do I handle this?

If I don't say anything you say I don't care
When I do say something or try to explain
myself whatever I say gets disregarded

Yes, we have disagreements but that happens
sometimes
We never mean what we say in the heat of
the moment

I'm confused and hurt
I don't know how to handle this

I want us to get better don't you want that?
I want to believe me when I tell you that I love
and care for you
Will you believe that?
I try to show you that I love and care for you
It's never going to be enough, will it?
I just don't know to do

Once told me

My mother once told me
Don't trust everybody, don't give your heart
to just anybody
But I didn't listen
I gave my heart to someone who didn't really
love me but only loved the thought of me
I trusted people who were unfaithful
and ignorant
So, what can I do now when I did the one thing,
she told me not to do?
I try again but this time
I have people earn my trust
I put lock on my heart until the right person
finds the key
This time I'll listen

The Girl

I act like a tough girl but I'm really a softy
I care if my family or friends get hurt

I'm the girl who is real down to earth underneath
all the things' people say I am
Pretty
Cute Ugly
Mean Sweet
Smart Dumb
Weird Freak
But really much more than that

I'm the girl that once you get to know me you
will love me or not
I'm the type of girl that can be on the phone
with anyone and talk for hours abut nothing
The girl who gets along with everybody
The girl who sings and dances when nobody is
listening or watching

The girl that can be myself around family
and friends
Goof off and act crazy and not care
The girl who you can talk to anything about
The girl who has feelings and can be sensitive
at times

Heart that won't quit

You say you don't love or care about him
Is that true?
When you see him with his friends
You think I miss that
When you see him with another girl you think
that used to be us or that should be me
It's obvious you care
You miss him
You love him
You care more than you think you do
Do you tell him how you feel?

You tell you love him
You miss him
You care about him more than you think
You miss the time y'all shared together
You tell him you want him back
But he doesn't feel the same he moved on

You think yourself is he really happy or is it just
for show?
It hurts but then you see how happy he is
and realize
You just have a heart that won't quit

Hurtful Lessons

I love you
The hardest and scariest thing you can say
to somebody or hear from somebody
When you love someone, it's supposed to be
a happy experience right?
You just know that person feels the same way
So, you say it
And you get hurt
Not hurt in the sense of they don't say it back
because they do feel the same
You get hurt in other ways
They start talking to somebody else and at first
you think it's nothing
Then they post pictures with said person so you ask
"Oh, is that person around when I'm not?"
They say "Yea but don't worry about them."
So, you brush it off
Then the slips up happen
Then they tell you they want a break but
the bad part is
That other person? That's the person they run
to on said "break"
And what do you do? You stay and get hurt
even more
I will never be that girl again
So, I'm not going to say those words unless
it's real

I refuse to look stupid again
But it was a lesson and because of that lesson
I have a lock on my heart until I find
the right person to unlock it

Doubtful Love

Why do I feel like maybe love isn't for me
right now?
I know what I want and I don't ask for much
Either somebody can't give what I want
from them
Or somebody tries to give me what I want
but I don't want them in that way
Then I start to think is it me?

Am I not opening enough?
Am I not vocal about what I want?
Did I already meet my person?
Did I miss my chance with somebody already?
I don't know but I know I'm patient

I'm working on myself right now and making
sure I'm happy with myself
If he comes in my life now or if he already
is in my life, I'm ready to be loved as
I'm learning to love myself
I'm ready to grow and build as I'm growing
and building myself

Do You?

Do you know I'm here for you?
Do you know that I believe in you?
Do you know that I care about you?
I mean do you even want to talk to me or see me?
Do you even think about me?
Do you miss me?
Well, I guess we'll never know
Since you won't talk to me

Hard to do

All I wanna do is see you
All I wanna is hold you
All I wanna do is kiss you
Why is that so hard to do?
Why do you make this so hard to do?

All I wanna do is be with you
Spend time with you
Laugh with you
Just be with you
Why is this so hard to do?

Like do you even wanna see me or anything?
If that's the case, why am I still here?
Do you feel the same way I do?

Do you wanna kiss me?
Do you wanna just chill and spend time with me?
Why is this so hard for you to do?

Asking for too much

I just want to feel your touch
Hear your voice when you say you miss me
Feel your arms around me when I'm sleep
I just want to be around you
Is that asking for too much?
I just want you to make me forget about
everything
Even if it only for a few hours
But I guess that's asking for too much right?

Too much

I don't ask for much
A kiss to shut me up
A hug to make me feel safe
Is that too much?

Show me you care
A call when you're bored
A text saying, I love you
Is that too much?

A look of admiration
Spend time with me
Is that too much?

Feels like maybe

Feels like I'm ignoring the signs that I should
walk away
Maybe I care too much to walk away
Maybe my feelings got involved
Maybe it hurts to walk away
Maybe I keep giving you the benefit of the doubt
Maybe the good outweighs the bad
Maybe
Maybe I'm just going through the motions

Feels like I'm wasting my time
Feels like you don't care
Feels like you're not here

Feels like maybe you won't notice when
I'm not there

Wonder

I wonder if it's enough
I wonder if I'm doing enough
How else can I show you that I'm here?
That I care?

Do I have to bug you?
Do I have to blow up your phone up?
Do I have to catch an attitude for you to reply?
Do I have to just wait until you realize that
I'm for you to open up?

I wonder

Should I give up?
Should I take a step back from us?
At this point is there a us?
I don't even know what to think or feel

Do I want you? Yes
Do I love you even if I never said it? Yes
Do I want us? Yes
But
Is it worth not talking to you for days? No
Is it worth not seeing you for months? No
Is it worth it at all? I honestly don't know

Letting Go

How do you walk away from a situation if you
already checked out emotionally?
I have tried
I have waited for you to make a change
I have told you what I wanted and needed from you

I know what I want from you
But maybe what I want is something you can't
give me and honestly that's fine
I shouldn't have to tell you what I want from you
time and time again because time and time
again nothing changes

I want, need and deserve more
Maybe you can't give that to me
Maybe you aren't ready for what I need you to be
Maybe I shouldn't have waited this long
to realize that
But I do know it's time for me to let myself
be open and ready to receive what I need
Even if that means letting you go

Miscommunication

One thing I hate to do is express my feeling
For me that's just hard for me to do
I have had promises broken
My hopes up just to be disappointed
My feelings hurt just because I didn't or couldn't
live up to your exceptions of me

I tell you that I know that you can't give me
what I want
That's fine. It took me a while to realize that
Now I do and it seems like you can't handle it

Don't wait for me
I have waited long enough
Waited for you to change
To communicate
To really get to know me
To understand me

I know people go thru things and sometimes
distant themselves
But don't ghost me then come back and expect
things to go back to normal
Maybe you can't handle a relationship
But don't do anything for me just because that's
what I told you I wanted

Take me out because you wanna
spend time together
Call me because you just wanna hear my voice
Ask me questions because you wanna know how
my mind works
Learn my love language so you know how
to connect with me

Man maybe in today's world I'm asking for much
I'll just wait until I get sent the right person,
I'm still young
I wish you the best though

Young love

This is why I never get too close to anyone
I'm either getting played or ignored
They just don't care
I'm only needed when they want something
from me
They just end up leaving

It's like every-time I open up to someone
I'm the one getting hurt
I just need to truly find myself

Last time I told somebody I loved them
He was in love with somebody else
Maybe I was young, dumb and "in love"

What is love?

What is love?
Love is a verb
Love is a noun
It's more than that It's a feeling
People have different views of love
To me it's a deeper emotion
Love is when one person can make you
feel better just by their presence
Love is trust
Love is caring about somebody
and their well-being
Love is more than a word
A noun A verb
Love is a feeling you can't explain
Love is special
Love isn't how it is in books
Love is hard Being in love is hard
Love hurts Its not supposed to break you
If does then it's not real, pure and true love
Being in love is a deep emotion shared
by two people
Being in love with the right person
It's beautiful It's a beautiful feeling
It's beautiful sight to see
With the right person Being in love feels right
This is just my opinion
I never been in love I hope I get to experience
being in love one day

This Love

Heart pounding fast
Hands sweaty
Butterflies inside
Are you the reason for this?

When I see you
I can't say anything
When I try the words don't sound right
If I tell you how I feel
Will you feel the same or walk away?
You tell me how you feel
You feel the same
There this thing that always happens when I see you

Heart pounding fast
Hands sweaty
Butterflies inside
Only because you are the reason
For
This love

Embrace or Run?

When you know you love do you run from it or
do you embrace it?

You run from it because you are scared you
might get hurt
You run because you've been hurt
You run because it's a new feeling
You run because you don't know how to handle it

But

You embrace it because it feels good
Embrace it because it makes you happy
Embrace it because you he says your name
you get butterflies
Embrace it because his voice makes you smile

It's okay to be scared and embrace it
Just know if the love is real nothing will tear
you apart
They will always be there no matter what
You will do whatever you can to make
that person happy

Love is strong
Love is pure
Love is happiness
Love is beautiful

Wish for Love

I want a love so genuine that I get butterflies
A love so pure I'm just happy to be around you
A love so real we can talk about anything
without judgement
A love that makes me comfortable enough to be
my true self
A love so raw that even in my worst moments
you still call me beautiful
A love so honest I can tell you all my secrets
A love so trusting that I can tell you
my biggest regret
A love that just makes me feel wanted
no matter what

SECTION 4

Acceptance

3:40 AM Crave

Up all night
Thoughts racing about everything
I'm torn
How do you crave something but also want
to be completely still and quiet?
How do you want something so bad you can
see it as clear as day but also afraid of change?

I crave change
I crave peace and quiet
I crave a better future
You can have anything in the world but only
want peace and a better life
Why?

I crave the feeling of taking a deep breath
in a space
An area
An environment
That's completely mines to have
I crave that feeling of accomplishment
I crave that inner feeling of serenity

I know it will happen
It's God's plan for; me to always have
what I crave

One window

One window is all I need to
Guide me to my dreams
Overcome my fears
Believe in love
Fall in love
Look into my future
Believe in myself
To succeed in life
One window is all I need to survive
This crazy thing called
Life

Insecure

The definition of insecure is not confident or assured
It also means uncertain, anxious or self-conscious
At some point we all feel insecure about something
Our bodies
Relationships
Jobs
Friendships

But what does insecure really mean?

I may not like how my stomach looks but I'm comfortable
and happy in my body
I may not wear tight clothes or swimsuits in the summer
but I'm comfortable in my skin
I'm not a size 2 or 4 and I don't plan to be anything less than a 12

Today's society has an image of how people should look
That makes our youth feel or become insecure
No image or person should another person feel insecure
If somebody thinks they have the authority to do that
Then that person is insecure themselves
Don't let society dictate who you are
Who you want to be
What you want to be
How you want to look
It's YOUR LIFE
Nobody can tell you how to live
Show how SECURE you are
How COMFORTABLE you are in YOUR SKIN

Good Enough

Sometimes I wonder if I'm good enough
Am I good enough for that one person to be
there when I don't have anyone else?
Am I good enough to be loved for me and
not what I can offer?
Am I good enough to be accepted for me?
Am I good enough to be what you expect me
to be even tough it's an illusion?

I'm not good enough to live up to this world
exceptions
Nobody will ever live up to that
Will we ever be good enough?

I realized that
It doesn't matter because we are
You are
I AM GOOD ENOUGH
Someday
Somebody will be more than enough
We will be accepted
You will be accepted
I will be accepted
That's enough for me

Life

I heard once in a movie
"Life is like a box chocolate; you never know
what you're going to get"
Life is hard it's nothing like a box of chocolates
We can't pick who we live with, go to school
with or anything and just be happy
We were brought into this by our parents,
made by them
Not machines or mixed up with different
ingredients
We can't be brought and thrown away when
expired or have no more use
Our parents take care of us, protect us, right?
Some people treat kids like we can just be
thrown away or put back on a shelf
People hit kids or rape kids and think it's okay
or normal when it's not
That's not love or a form of love It's abuse
You don't treat people that way
Life is love, laughter, being able to do what
you want with no remorse
It's being able to say I Love You to someone
and mean it

Life is meaningful and has purpose
Having fights with friends and family,
relationships

Having people in your life that make you happy
You control your life
Nobody controls it for you
So, love life
Live it to the fullest
Don't let anyone stop you and always Stay true
to yourself

Distance

Sometimes you have to distance yourself
From people
From certain situations
Now that's not saying that you want to give up
It giving yourself space so you can better yourself
And to view things from a different and
clearer perspective

Gems

Despite what people say
Despite how many times you hear no
Despite how many failures you have
Keep going
Keep fighting
Keep doing what you love

No matter how many times you give up
No matter how many you lose inspiration
No matter how many mistakes you make
Keep going
Keep fighting
Keep doing what you love

While people may not understand or see
the vision
You see the vision
Just as clear as if it was right in front of you

Waiting

Waiting
Waiting for things to get better
Waiting for things to change for the better
Waiting for things to get less complicated

Waiting for something real
Waiting for us to happy with no complications
I'm just waiting

I know things will get better
I know we will be happy
Constantly
I'm ready
Are you ready?

Because it just seems like the universe is just
Waiting
For us

Speechless

How do I express myself when words don't come
to mind?
How do I express joy when I'm speechless?
I simply can't
I feel joy
A sense of relief
A happiness I can't and don't want to escape
A fullness in my heart that I never want
to go away
No tears of joy because tears just aren't enough
A love so deep in my heart that I can't express
Forever thankful
Forever blessed
Forever love

Happy

What does happiness mean to you?
Does your family make you happy?
Does that one person make you happy?
Does your job make you happy?

Happiness isn't just a feeling
It's an emotion
One compliment
One person
One phone call
Can make a bad day turn good
That can make you happy
I believe happiness is love
Love
Friendships
Family
Writing

I'm happy because I have people in my who love
and care about me
I'm happy I'm writing again
I'm not sure why I stopped
I'm happy I'm able to share my gift
And it not the end

ACKNOWLEDGEMENT

To all the people who helped me through this process, who inspired the poems, who helped me grow and learn those people are my family and friends who I love deep. To David who answered every annoying question I had and who created a visual for my book I only saw in my head I am forever happy and grateful for his help and work. This book is my baby in way but it was my way of healing and I hope it can help whoever reads it.

Thank you and I love all of my readers 3000!

ABOUT THE AUTHOR

Teisha Noble is a self-published writer and poet (speaking it into existence) She is from Philadelphia and started her journey of writing in high school. At first it was just way to express her creativity and because she enjoys it, she even wrote a screenplay but as she got older it become a way for share her feeling or just simply express herself when she felt she couldn't. These poems have in a way helped her cope with loss, heartbreak and everything in between and these poems even motivated her to start her own publishing company Writers Escape. You can follow this up-and-coming writer and on Instagram at @writersescapellc

www.ingramcontent.com/pod-product-compliance
Lightning Source LLC
LaVergne TN
LVHW050941080826
845145LV00004B/1354

* 9 7 8 1 7 3 7 2 9 2 5 0 0 *